Jillian Elizabeth

ENCHANTRESS TRINITY'S SECRET BOOK OF SPELLS

ENCHANTRESS TRINITY'S SECRET BOOK OF SPELLS

Jillian Elizabeth

This book is a work of fiction.

Shenanigans and good times are ahead inside this book.

Just remember you were warned!

Cover Design copyright © AWT Cover Design

Editing and proofreading by Virginia Tesi Carey

Formatting by JM Walker

"Quit hiding your magic, the world is ready for you."
~Danielle Doby

Welcome to the sweet little lair of Enchantress Trinity (her mom's kitchen).

She's ready to stir up some fun with you and show you all the fun she loves to have.

Trinity is a 9 year old girl that always makes life as fun as she can.

What do you like to do for fun?

GARDEN HERBS AND PLANTS

Let's take a look at the Enchantress' garden. Every healthy little witch, enchantress, warlock, mommy or daddy can use these items every day!

Aloe - *For luck and protection. Also good for scrapes and burns.*

Chamomile - *For sleep and resting.*

Clover - *For wealth and success. Maybe you can even catch a leprechaun.*

Honeysuckle - *Smells so pretty and makes your spirit feel good.*

Lavender - *Brings happiness and peace.*

Lilac - *Keep this with you for love.*

Lily - *Healthy healing.*

Marigold - *Keeps you protected.*

Poppy - *Helps for sleeping and love.*

Roses - *Healing and love.*

STONES AND CRYSTALS

Stones and Crystals help us to feel our most magical when we hold them or keep them near to us. Some of those magic stones and crystals can be found around your own house and you'd never even know!

Remember we all have the perfect power and magic inside of us if we believe we can use it. You are magical!

Amethyst (Violet color) - *A change in life.*

Rose Quartz (Pink color) - *Love and self-healing.*

Blue Lace Agate (Light Blue color with White in it) - *Healing*

Turquoise (Greenish-Blue color) - *A journey*

Citrine (Yellowish-Orange color) - *Celestial Wisdom*

Onyx (Black color) - *Absorbs Negative Energy*

Malachite (Bright Green color) - *Deep Healing and the power to protect.*

Jade (Green of different shades) - *Blessings*

Moonstone (Grayish-White color) - *Calm and Protection*

Emerald (Dark Green color) - *Good Fortune and Youth.*

Who's ready for some fun?!

Now we need to find something that you want to use as your magical wand.
Every boy and girl needs something they have that they believe is full of their secret magic.
It could be your favorite spoon you eat breakfast with.
It could be mom's best cooking spoon. She makes magical food for you with it right?
Anything you wish it to be, make it your magic.

FUN RECIPES

WARLOCK DRINK

~2 cups of orange juice
~ ½ cup of lemon juice
~ 4 cups of apple cider
~ 4 cups of white grape juice (sparkling)
~ dry ice

Mix them together and you'll have a fun drink that tastes good, and looks fun with the smoky effect.

Witches Brew

~Sherbert
~ 7-Up

Mix the fizzy goodness together and enjoy!

HOMEMADE CARAMEL SAUCE

~ 1 cup packed brown sugar
~ ½ cup butter
~ ¼ cup milk
~ 1 teaspoon vanilla extract

Bring brown sugar, butter, and milk to a gentle boil and cook until thickened for 1 to 2 minutes.
Remove from heat; add vanilla extract.

Dip apples or pour over ice cream and enjoy!

"Magic is believing in yourself. If you can do that, you can make anything happen."

~Unknown

Jillian Elizabeth

Witch Hat Treats

Big, chocolate and gooey fun, this Halloween treat both looks and tastes so good! Put your guests under a spell with this for sure!

~ 1 package (6oz.,1cup) semi-sweet chocolate morsels.

~3 tablespoons butter or margarine

~1 package (10oz., about 40) marshmallows/ or 4 cups of mini marshmallows

~6 cups rice crispies cereal

~Canned frosting or decorating gel

~Assorted candies

1. In a large saucepan melt chocolate morsels and butter over low heat.
2. Add marshmallows and stir until completely melted.
3. Remove from heat.
4. Add rice cereal. Stir until well coated.
5. Cool slightly.
6. Using buttered hands, shape a small amount of mix into a small circle. This will be the brim of your hat.
7. Shape a little bigger amount into a cone shape. This is the top of your witch hat.
8. You can secure both parts together with a toothpick to keep it together.
9. Decorate it with frosting and/or candies.

"Those who don't believe in Magic will never find it."
~Roald Dahl

Halloween Monster Apples

~2 green apples cut into 4 pieces

~Peanut butter or almond butter

~Sunflower seeds

~Strawberries sliced

~ Miniature marshmallows for eyes

~Small amount of black frosting for eyes

1. First, cut the middle out of each quarter of the apple in order to create a mouth.
2. Coat the inside of the gap you created for the mouth with peanut or almond butter
3. Place sunflower seeds on the underside of the top apple piece (inside mouth for top teeth).
4. Place a piece of sliced strawberry on the inside of the bottom apple slice (inside the mouth for the tongue).
5. Use a dab of peanut or almond butter on the very top of the apple. Place a mini marshmallow on each dab to hold the eyes in place.
6. Dab a small amount of black or whatever other color frosting you choose on the marshmallows for the pupils of the eye.
7. Have fun with your little apple monster. It's a fun treat no matter how old you are!

PUMPKIN MONSTER PUDDING CUPS

You'll need:

~Clear plastic cups

~Brownies

~Pumpkin flavored pudding

~Marshmallows (big size)

~Chocolate sauce

1. *Tear brownies apart and place in a bowl to the side.*
2. *Add a large spoonful of pumpkin pudding to bottom of cup.*
3. *Add a brownie layer on top of the pudding inside the cup.*
4. *Put another large spoonful of pudding on top of brownies inside the cup.*
5. *Now you have 3 layers and your Monster is yelling from his brownie mouth.*
6. *Add marshmallows to the top of pudding, placing a dab of chocolate sauce to each. These are your monster's eyeballs.*

Jillian Elizabeth

"It's important to remember that we all have magic inside us."
~JK Rowling

Please tell me you are having fun so far.
Did you make a silly mess yet?
Maybe a little bit?

Keep turning pages......the messy fun starts now!

Jillian Elizabeth

Colored Noodles

You'll need:

-Angel Hair or Spaghetti Noodles
- Zip Lock Freezer Bags
-Food Coloring

1. *Boil the noodles and drain*
2. *Separate Noodles into ziplock bags (1 bag per color)*
3. *20 drops of color (1 per bag) into each bag of Noodles*
4. *Zip the bags closed*
5. *Shakes each bag*
6. *Place bags in fridge for 10 minutes*
7. *Pull out of the fridge.*
8. *Mix all the colors in a bowl. You can play with them or just eat them*

PUMPKIN DECORATING

MUMMY PUMPKIN

-Gauze
-Tacky Glue
-Large Googly eyes
-Small Pumpkin

1. Squirt tacky glue all over your pumpkin
2. Grab and end of your gauze and begin to wrap it around your pumpkin
3. Make sure the gauze is on the glue and push it on a little
4. Use the tacky glue to glue on your mummy's eyes

MELTED CRAYON PUMPKIN

-*Pumpkin (white or orange)*
-*Crayons*
-*Tacky Glue*
-*Blow dryer*

1. *Unwrap your crayons*
2. *Cut the crayons in half*
3. *Glue about 16 crayon pieces using tacky glue to the pumpkin in different spots*
4. *After the glue has dried, use a hair dryer to melt the crayons*
5. *The crayons will start to drip down the sides of the pumpkin as it melts.*
6. *Melt to your liking*

A Messy Good Time

Pumpkin Putty

-¾ teaspoons of Borax
-1 ½ cups of very warm water
-White School Glue
-Orange Food Coloring
-Pumpkin Pie Spice

1. Combine the water and Borax in a small bowl
2. In a second bowl, combine
    -2 cups of white school glue
    -1 ½ cups of very warm water
    -5-10 drops of orange Food Coloring
    - 1-2 tsp. of pumpkin pie spice
3. Mix the contents of both bowls well, and then combine both bowls

As the ingredients of both bowls are mixed, the pumpkin putty will start to form. Work the rest of the puttu by kneading by hand.

Can't you smell all the pumpkin pie goodness?!

Jillian Elizabeth

Pretend Snot Slime

-4 oz of Glitter Glue
-⅛ cup of liquid starch
-5-10 drops of Food Coloring (yellow or green)
-¼ tsp. of Borax
-Water

1. Dump the glue into a bowl
2. Fill the empty glue container with water and dump it into the bowl
3. Mix until the glue is watery
4. Add the liquid starch and keep stirring
5. The mix will start to thicken
6. Add the small amount of Borax for easier clean-up
7. Put your Food Coloring in and mix until your snot slime is just the right color for you
8. Bottle it up and gross out all your friends and family!

FREAK OUT ICE CUBES

-Fake bugs
-Ice Trays

1. Place a fake bug in the bottom of each ice tray
2. Fill each ice tray with water until bugs are covered
3. Place in freezer

When you put these in your family and friend's drinks they will scream with delight!!

SKITTLE PAINTING

-*Big bag of Skittles candy*
-*Corn Syrup*
-*5 Small Containers*

1. *Separate your colors of Skittles by placing each of the colors in its own cups. About 25 of each color in its cup*
2. *Pour the corn syrup over the Skittles until they are completely covered*
3. *Watch the fun begin as the color starts to lift from the Skittles. Give it a few hours to really get the color moving*
4. *When the corn syrup is nice and colorful in each cup, stir it up with a paintbrush in each color.*
5. *Your paint smells so good right? Give your paint a sniff and let the painting fun begin!*

You will notice how shiny it is even after it dries, your new paintings will even smell great!
The best part is it's safe to have a small taste.

MASON JAR MAGIC AQUARIUM

-Aquarium gravel
-Small seashells
-Cheap plastic plants
-Plastic Sea Creatures
-Mason Jars
-Blue Food Coloring
-Submersible LED Light
-Water Resistant Glue

1. Using the water resistant glue, glue the submersible LED light to the underside of the mason jar top
2. Fill the bottom of the mason jar with the aquarium gravel
3. Place the small seashells in the gravel at the bottom
4. Put the aquarium plants in and push it into the gravel so it's secure
5. Fill the mason jar up with water
6. Drop about 5-10 drops of blue food coloring into the water. You can use more if you want it to be a darker blue
7. Put the sea creatures into your jar and see how pretty they look inside
8. Turn the light to on
9. Screw the lid back on the jar tightly

Look at your beautiful creation! Best of all you don't have to feed these creatures and you can still love them.

Jillian Elizabeth

Magical Dragon Eggs

-Styrofoam Egg
-Flat Silver Thumbtacks
-Shimmery Nail Polish (any color you wish)

1. Using the thumbtacks, start at the bottom of the eggs and make a line of thumbtacks all around the egg.
2. Be careful not to poke yourself and make sure an adult is doing this with you.
3. Overlap the thumbtacks on the next row so they rest over the first row you made. Go around the whole egg again.
4. Repeat this with each line until the egg is covered in the thumbtacks which represent your scales.
5. Paint your shimmer nail polish over the thumbtacks. Make your dragon's scales really stand out.
6. Let dry. Try to stand it up for better drying on all sides without smudging.

Look how beautiful your pretend dragon egg is!

MAGIC BOTTLES

-Glass or plastic bottles with screw tops
-Water
-Baby Oil
-Glitter
-Metallic Confetti

1. Add water to the bottles until they're about ¾ full.
2. Pour 10-20 drops of baby oil in each bottle.
3. Add glitter and confetti to each bottle and replace the tops.
4. Shake your bottle to make the magic happen.

Watch all the pretty colors and bubbles inside your magical bottle!

Jillian Elizabeth

GALAXY OF MAGIC IN A JAR

-Silver Glitter
-Cotton Balls
-Mason Jars
-Acrylic Paints
-Water
-Plastic Cups
-Wood Stick to Stir

1. Put water in cups (half full)
2. Add paint color to each cup of water- mix to see how much paint you want to use depending on the brightness of color.
3. Fill bottom part of jar with cotton balls.
4. Put glitter on top of cotton- shake around.
5. Choose one cup of paint color/water mix and pour slowly into jag on cotton. Be careful not to fill too much. Just so the cotton is colored fully.
6. Add another layer of cotton balls on top of that first color.
7. Put your glitter again on that layer of cotton balls.
8. Choose your second color of paint/water mix and pour over the cotton. Just enough to cover that layer of cotton in color.
9. Add another layer of cotton balls on top of the second color.
10. Glitter that layer of cotton balls.
11. Choose your third and final paint color/water mix.
12. Pour the paint/water mix enough to cover that layer of cotton.
13. Place the top on the jar and screw it shut.

Look at the pretty layers of colors and sparkle that looks like a galaxy in space full of colorful swirls and twinkling stars!

You are doing such a great job and I'm so very proud of you!

BATH BOMB

-Baking Soda
-Citric Acid
-Epsom Salts
-Water
-Essential Oils
-Olive Oil
-Food Coloring
-Bowl
-Whisk
-Jar
-Cupcake Papers
-Cupcake Pan

1. 1 cup of baking soda
2. ½ cup of Citric acid
3. ½ cup of Epsom salts
4. 1 tsp. Water
5. 2 tsp. Essential oil (any scent you choose)
6. 3 tsp. olive oil
7. 10-20 drops of food coloring (any color you choose
8. Mix in a bowl with the spoon and whisk until well mixed
9. Place cupcake papers in cupcake pans
10. Pour mix into each paper until almost filled
11. Let sit and mixture will harden

Now with your next bath drop it in the water and watch it fizz, turn the water color, smell so good and feel so soft when you sit in the bath water.

Remember every little magical creature needs their rest!

Jillian Elizabeth

Temporary Hair Color for Kids

-Kool Aid (color of your choosing)
-¼ cup of hair conditioner or mayonnaise
-1 tbsp. White vinegar for longer lasting color
-Plastic or rubber gloves
-Paint brush, Water bottle or Old Ketchup bottle
-Plastic Wrap

1. Put on your gloves on to protect your hands from staining.
2. Mix the Kool-Aid, hair conditioner or mayonnaise and vinegar into a bowl.
3. Place color in water bottle, leave in bowl or old Ketchup bottle.
4. If using the bowl then use the paintbrush to paint the color on your hair.
5. If using the bottles then spray or squirt on hair.
6. When color is added as you wish, wrap hair in plastic wrap.
7. Wait 60 minutes, set timer.
8. Rinse your hair and wash as normal.
9. Color should last 3 to 5 shampoos.

How does it look? Fabulous like you?!

KINETIC SAND

-1 cup of sand
-½ tbsp. cornstarch
-1 tsp. dish soap
-Water

1. In a big bin or container combine the play sand and cornstarch- mix well.
2. In a separate container- combine the soap and water.
3. Stir until the water is bubbly.
4. Slowly pour the water into the sand/cornstarch and mix well.
5. Mix and mix- add more water as needed.
6. Continue to mix and add water until the desired consistency is reached of not sticky.
7. Usually just a ¾ cup of water added is sufficient.

Don't forget to have fun with the sand! It's magical and doesn't stick to you.

Jillian Elizabeth

FAIRY POTION

-Water
-Glitter
-Flowers or flower petals

1.   Mix them together to make your potion

For more fun you can pour in to ice cube trays and freeze.
Your ice will be fun to watch melt, and smell so good!
Just don't put it in a drink......YUCK!

BUBBLE FOAM

-Tear Free Bubble Bath
-Water
-Food Coloring
-Hand Mixer

1. Use in bathtub for the best fun
2. Add 2 parts of water for 1 part bubble bath(½ cup of water and ¼ cup of bubble bath
3. Add your favorite color food coloring
4. Mix until it's fluffy and fun!!!

Climb in and have your own bubbly foam party!

Jillian Elizabeth

FAIRY FIZZ

-Baking Soda
-Vinegar
-Dish Soap
-Powder Paint (or food coloring)
-Glitter Flakes (or glitter)
-Small glass jar
-Spoon
-Tray or large dish

1. Fill the small jar halfway with vinegar.
2. Stir in a spoonful of your chosen color.
3. Add a big squeeze of dish soap and a little glitter.
4. Place the jar on the tray or large dish.
5. Put in a spoonful of baking soda into the jar.
6. Say, "Yes to Mess," and watch the magic happen.

You should see it all fizz and bubble right out of the top of the jar. This was a fun little science activity!

Magic Fairy Dough

-1 cup of hair conditioner (scented is fun)
-2 ½ cups of cornstarch (dry)
-Food Coloring (any color)
-Bowl
-Spoon

1. Using a spoon, mix the hair conditioner and cornstarch together. If the mix is too wet then add some more cornstarch.
2. Knead the dough together.
3. Put in 10-20 drops of food coloring, any color you choose.

Your magical dough is ready to be played with and sniffed if you added the scented conditioner.

WITCH POTION

-Vegetable Oil-Food Coloring

-Water

-Alka-Seltzer

-A tall bottle with cap or cork

-Funnel

1. Fill your bottle ¾ of the way full with vegetable oil.
2. Fill the rest of the way with water (leave room about 1 inch from the top).
3. Add food coloring of your choice.
4. Break Alka-seltzer into 4 pieces and drop 1 piece into the bottle.

Watch it bubble and brew with all the power you've put into it!

"Reach as high as you can, and then reach a little higher. There you will find magic and possibility, and maybe even cookies."
~ Marc Johns

Jillian Elizabeth

Fun Spells

Sharing Spell

Have friends that weren't taught to share? Have no fear they're no worse for wear.
All you need is a piece of hair, a pinch of salt and underwear!

Make the sound of a donkey mare- tap your wand on a pear.
Now give it to your friend to share, they will so love that you care.

MEAN TEACHER SPELL

Have a teacher you want to be nice?
All it takes is a little spice.

A pinch of cinnamon thrown into the air, tap your wand to your hair.

Now twirl around and touch your chair- point to your teacher and yell- Be fair!

Now this may make your teacher stare.
But do not, do not, do not share!

QUIET SPELL

Are you needing a moment of peace?

Try this spell to find release.

If someone is noisy like geese, touch your nose and yell- Maurice!

Now wiggle your toes, strike a pose because shhhhhh no one knows that you froze their clothes.

They will be in such a shock, their lips will give themselves a lock.

Annoying Parent Spell

Parents bugging about this and that? Wish you had a magical cat? Well let's do something about that.

Jump 3 times in the air, stomp your right foot without a care.

Twirl around, point you magic wand at your offending parent.
Squint your eyes and yell- Surprise!

They will be so surprised, they just may leave you alone.

Jillian Elizabeth

ACKNOWLEDGEMENTS

To Trinity Marie, for being the amazing kid you are. For the many great years you've made me laugh, and continue to be so proud of you.

Keep dancing, being the sweet girl you always have been, and just keep smiling that pretty smile of yours.

For all the help from Trinity, Sofie, Becca and Aaron for ideas and input on our fun little book!

Every kid that enjoys this story, thank you for having fun with me!

Printed in Great Britain
by Amazon